Look What I Found!

In the Garden

Paul Humphrey

FRANKLIN WATTS
LONDON•SYDNEY

This edition 2009

Franklin Watts
338 Euston Road
London NW1 3BH

Franklin Watts Australia
level 17/207 Kent Street
Sydney NSW 2000

Planning and production by Discovery Books Limited
Editor: Geoff Barker
Designer: Ian Winton
Natural history consultant: Michael Chinery
Language consultant: Helen Barden
Photographer: Chris Fairclough

Additional photographs: Michael Chinery: 6/7b, 7t; Bruce Coleman:
11 (Felix Labhardt), 13 (Kim Taylor), 14, 19 (Hans Reinhard), 16 (Jane Burton);
FLPA/Foto Natura: 24; NHPA: 15, 17 (Stephen Dalton); OSF/Photolibrary.com:
22; PhotoDisc: 8, 27; Alex Ramsay: front cover, back cover, title page.

A CIP catalogue record for this book is available from the
British Library

ISBN 978 0 7496 8913 1

Dewey decimal classification number: 577.5'54

Printed in China

Franklin Watts is a division of Hachette Children's Books,
an Hachette UK Company.
www.hachette.co.uk

Contents

I went into the garden and this is what I found. Lots of sweet-smelling, bright flowers...

and trees in blossom.

Bees were buzzing from flower to flower. They were looking for pollen and nectar.

I saw this hover-fly.
It looked a lot like a bee.

Down on the lawn I found some
daisies. The petals had pink tips.

By the fence, an earthworm slid by.

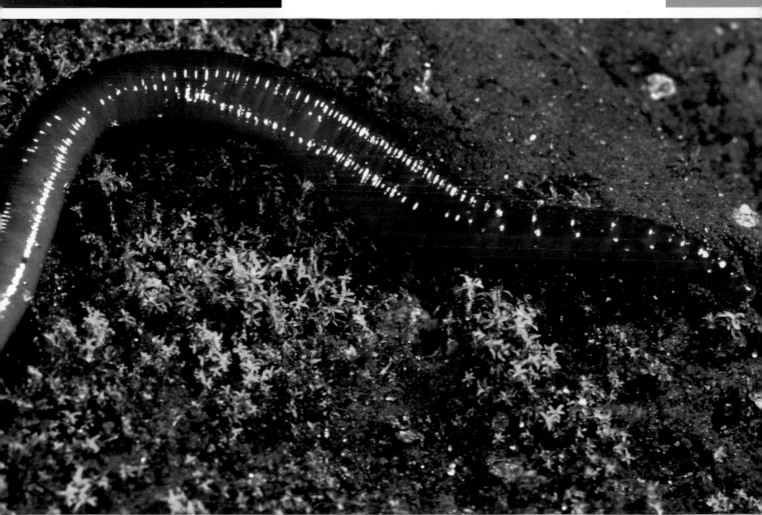

A sparrow was singing among these yellow flowers...

and a blue tit flew by with a
caterpillar in its beak.

There was a centipede on
a piece of tree bark.

Can you count all its legs?

This earwig
was crawling
on a flower.
Earwigs have
six legs.

A spider had made a beautiful web to catch food.

This fly had better watch out!

Dad told me that this pile
of earth was a molehill.

The mole had pushed the earth
out when it dug its tunnel.

Mum doesn't like weeds, but
these dandelions at the bottom
of the garden were pretty.

I found one with a seed
head. I blew the seeds away.

Look at these snails' eggs.

Snails are pests in
the garden, but
they are food
for birds.

23

A caterpillar was munching
on some leaves.

Soon it will turn into
a butterfly...

just like this small
tortoiseshell butterfly.

I planted some sunflower seeds.

I hope they
grow into tall plants.

I had fun exploring my garden.

Now it was time to go inside.

Can you find these in the book?

hover-fly

sparrow

daisy

28

butterfly

snail

dandelions

29

Index

DR

Lo
WI
I Fou